Coláiste Mhuire Gan Smál
Luimneach
D1428851

THE SPEAKING STONES

Peter Fallon

The Speaking Stones

Drawings by Timothy Engelland

MIC LIBRARY
WITHDRAWN FROM STOCK

Gallery Books

13472

The Speaking Stones
is published simultaneously
in paperback and in a
clothbound limited edition
of 300 copies signed by the author.

The Gallery Press
19 Oakdown Road
Dublin 14
Ireland.

© Peter Fallon 1978

All rights reserved

ISBN 0 902996 72 X *(clothbound)*
0 902996 73 8 *(paperback)*

Coláiste Oideachais
Mhuire Gan Smál
Luimneach
Class No. 819.1914
Acc. No. 31,781
FAL

Cover design by Timothy Engelland

Contents

Acknowledgements

I thank the trustees of Deerfield Academy in Massachusetts where I was poet-in-residence in 1976-77.

Acknowledgements are due to the editors of *Albany Road* (Massachusetts), *The Antioch International Review, The Bellingham Review, Broadsheet, Contraband* (Maine), *The Drumlin, Hibernia, The Honest Ulsterman, Icarus, Irish University Review, The Journal of Irish Literature, The Mare Near You* (Goshen, Indiana), *Mississippi Valley Review, The Nantucket Review, New Poetry: Cork Examiner, Poets in Focus* (New York), *Resurgence* (London), *River Bottom* (Wisconsin) and *Soundings 1974* (edited by Seamus Heaney) where most of these poems first appeared.

Many of them were included in *A Gentler Birth* (1976), *Victims* (1977) and *Finding the Dead* (1978) and published in limited editions, with drawings by Timothy Engelland, by the Deerfield Press, Massachusetts.

I have read many of these poems in Ireland, America and Canada and thank the organisers of these readings.

The Speaking Stones are in Farnaglough, near Oldcastle, in Co. Meath. They were shown to me first by Tom Ward who's 94.

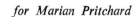

for Marian Pritchard

One

Walking in woodland
I find an egg among feathers and bone,
immediate death
and a gentler birth
than a lamb's whose eyes

the crows had picked this morning
before its two feet touched the ground
as a ewe wondered
what labour happened
to herald that doom behind her left shoulder.

I take a thorn and pierce each end,
blow
the yolk on the ground like a petal of gorse,
spilt gold,
and hold a bubble of bone.

I bring this to you in the city,
a handsel, a token,
this and a prayer your beginnings
be smooth as its skin,
soft as the down, innocent as lambs'.

The Making of Paths

As random as naming
the making of paths begins.
They wobble a drunken way in snow,
recover, as faithful to ends
as cattle to courses of underground streams.

They knot like hair.
One follows one and finds
it's one twin end of Y.
They unwind like a story.
Like a lazy wind they won't go round.

They lapse in woods
but overflow the open ground,
splashes of prints that spill
from the parcel of paths we bring with us
to empty here and there.

Three

Where three fields meet
there's good water —
strong as forge-water
it makes you well.

Dreamed three times
the dream is true
though three times three bells
knell a man
and three times two a woman.

North of here
they'll tie two boats together
that none might be
the third to leave the harbour.

In 1914 in the New Forest
an old woman was not surprised
for all the Spring and Summer
her people counted overhead
the wild swans fly in threes and threes.

Nettle

does not sting
like some crazed bee
drunk with revenge.
The seedwine cures

a mad dog's bite,
revives from nightshade,
hemlock, mandrake-root.
A neighbouring dock,

cool enough to conserve butter,
dulls the freckling,
tempers local fever.
Wasteland flower

will not wound.
Bend the leaf-hairs
spilling pain:
it's *you* that sting.

Waterfall

Do not expect
to know one.
Ice is a mood
that will not last.

Slow hums remind
that water falls into itself,
a ragged rope of roaring
wind and miles diminish.

Falling. Waterstream
and pool contribute,
a moment neither this nor that,
until the pool and stream take back.

Colaiste Oideachais Mhuire Gan Smal
Luimneach

Gravities

1
Behind the moving herds
down roads the collies sulk,
their tongues as long and limp
as tails unrolled across their

teeth. The townland echoes
to these moves, the stampede
like a stream into the estuary
of fields. At open gates

they jump over nothing
and land on their feet.

2
They have been long in the yards,
the split of their feet awkward
on cobbles, or chewing the cud
of a long afternoon, when another drive

begins. They go the longest route.
By dogs they're defiant and scared.
Their lives are in turmoil
and they straggle to eat,

to stuff their five stomachs
for safety or sentence.

3
A ewe moves northward
to a gate, her lambs in tow.
Another follows and again
the night's migration

is begun. Thin lines of sheep
approach a slope, the frantic calls
resume, the mothers' for lambs,
the lambs' for milk.

And I've known men
tell weather by this moment.

4
There's always one the drovers miss,
one that disdains the rush
to follow, that dozes by walls,
wool shaded like granite,

a grain that remains in the upper glass
to measure their absence for dipping
or dosing, a ploy that backfires —
in minutes she's scanning the field,

nudging the gate. She just restores
her dignity, recovers to greet the others'
    return.

5
She yeaned outside and unattended
sometime before day broke
and takes the lambs to be her own
like luggage she won't question

and will defend a while,
will stand up for and stamp her foot for,
but as a farm is made of fields
and fences, fearlessness is bound.

Soon she shies to merge with others,
leaves lambs and footmarks on the ground.

6 *The Deer*
They rise as one, fear like respect.
A step on greensward brings a bolt.
Breaking this way, breaking that,
they wheel together as a hare

around a hill and, as a hare,
sit up and stare for what the wind began,
and then bound this way, then bound that,
around the park they hold in trust

to stay alone, as hare or hermit,
far from the harming or helping hand.

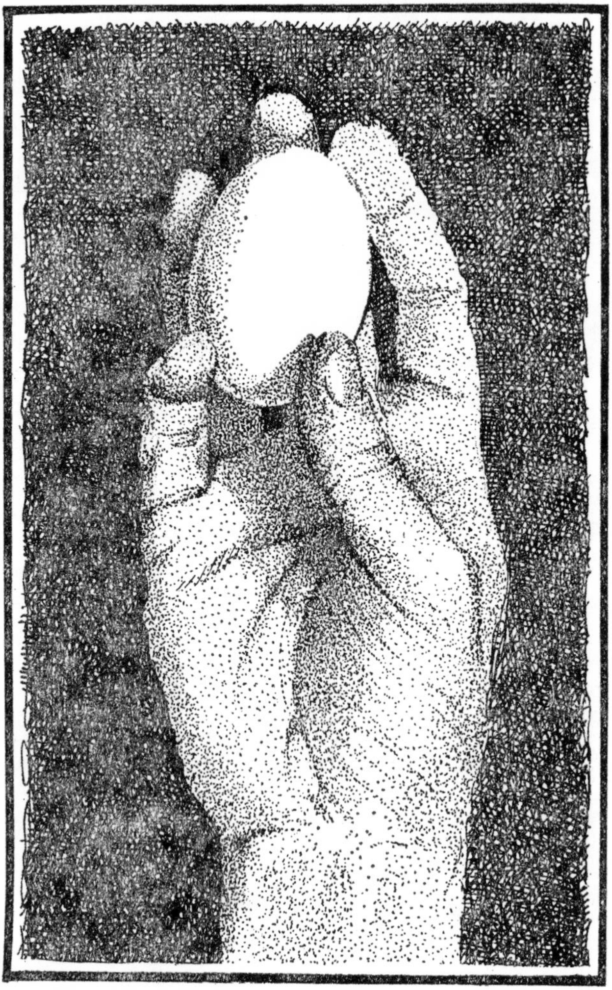

Collie

No rutting hare's
as mad as Polo.
He'll wrestle stones,

chase birds
and not let go
a stick you throw

until he knows it's dead.
He's there eleven years
my cousin multiplies by seven

to age a dog.
Young pups come in
but he hangs round the back —

sticks and stones
the last rats that he'll catch,
the last strays that he'll round.

Cards

Because she was
the woman of the house
and disapproved of drink,
when she thought fit
she wet the tea,
nor did she care for cards:
her spouse would bet a farm
of land as soon as spit.

Still cards were played
at Lennoxbrook, especially
whist. The neighbours drove
for miles to wage for fun.
Young Frank studied his hand
and looked oppressed.
How many tricks had he?
'If I'd another I'd have one!'

One night Pat Mullion cried
'Oh Clare' toward his wife,
slumped forward on green baize
and breathed no more.
Shock turned to laughter, then
to shame. A night of prayer
and praise began, tense talk
of all a moment holds in store.

The village pub was poker house
until a hand revealed six cards
and Hughie said 'That's it'
as grown men rebelled and rowed
for pennies. Too many lost
too much too frequently
in their wild urge to play,
to be part of a crowd.

So the packs were put away;
the dreams of winning pots
dissolved. Men turned
again to talk and darts.

Intelligence of rain and parish lore,
Pat Timmons saying songs,
the games of 301—bull's eyes
deposed the king and queen of hearts.

And now we play for more than money,
local fame. Sometimes we cheat
and sometimes improvise the rules
we risk such desparate stakes:
to love and live. Sometimes
the cards we play aren't those
we're dealt and always we contend
our darker hands dealers' mistakes.

Letting the Pond Go

My grandfather created
a crocodile
to keep us from the water
but where it went
the day decided
no one ever answered.

It was always midsummer
in the shade
of beech and drooping ash
the day that half the county called,
the sluice turned open
and the pond streamed through.

Excitement shapes peculiar skill
and the fish that slipped
from hands were held
by others or a net.

Like knots of danger
eels were kept
in the onflow
in a nail-punched barrel.

In a good harvest each company
took home a bucket filled with trout.

Bad luck and worse winters —
the fish disappeared in overgrowth.

My uncle planned to breed again
and introduced the first.
A heron heard
and parked itself on Reilly's side.

Remembering an old story
of how a heron's heart is weak
my uncle stood on ours
and roared to shock
        until he was hoarse.

An oak of indifference,
the heron picked them one by one.

There are no fish now
and we've all outgrown the crocodile.
The weeds are back
and yet that bird's legbone
serves no one that we know
    for pipe.

Mole

Thalidomide, earth-seal
of muscle, tail a teat
and nose the sound of stone,
you wing your way, rootmonger,

grubbing on what directed mission.
Your hungers drive you to attack
even your own, untender lover,
blindlike, palms forever open.

Spading raw earth
your velvet drains whole counties
scenting those only homes
that crumbling surrender to you.

Hedgehog

Some obscure time
along the riding
their urchin snores
bring fox or gipsy
to their keep.

All year the boar
pads out for seeds.
One made his way
into our henhouse,
ate himself too big to leave.

Blood calls to blood,
another climbed a concrete wall
as a night-blue badger
broke a chain
and left a shed we don't know how.

I think the old ones whiten
and hear them say
'I am the glad outsider.
The long sleep is my alibi.
I go alone
by the way of things

nimbling by
the forest-edge,
garden hedge or river-bend.
I do not need a lie
or legend to survive.
To eat I come out and to die.'

Colaiste Oideachais Mhuire Gan Smal
31,781
Luimneach

A Dream of Heaven

Its hams were hung in rustic stores
and larders long ago
and people christened it
uneven leggèd it went so.

By Loughcrew church each evening
a burly brock flatfoots
the well-worn ways to water,
bashing past bushes, under roots

and through thorn wire.
It excavates new galleries,
digs pits for dung and hones
its claws on old oak trees.

It bundles with forepaws
the bedding for a birth,
hugs hay, soft moss, wild bloom.
Say bawson, brock, earth-

pig, a badger is a yard of grey
in a sphere of black and white
whose sow mates from
her second summer on for life,

faithful as wolves.
She's true as this to home;
the sett in which she lives
will be in time her tomb.

But twilights with her boar
she rummages for nuts and all
kinds of grasses, for marybuds and
berries and codlings knocked by squalls.

They mark their range by musking,
leave known smells to track
on stumps and stones and fencing-
posts as they go homing back

to their share of the world,
their suckling cubs, a murmur
of whelps that surfaced once
when I was there.

Then in my wonder grew
a dream of heaven
and out into the holy day
came all the creatures

of the dark and underground,
came all beings untimidly,
and in its light their lives
were floreate and full.

Genesis

In the beginning were six
cows we knew by name
and genealogy;
we milked by hand.
I argued for a bull,
to keep a handsome scrub.

You'd almost wish in innocence
to have one trespass dew-damp clover
to see my uncle's famous trick.
He'd pick the spot, stab,
then light escaping gas
to jet the beast to health again.

Till Mickey Kelly called.
That man possessed the way of it.
He knew the feel, the weight of it,
how tight to make the strings;
the cuts to draw he knew
but never settled to their cry.

That was always more, louder.
Yet he'd a job to do,
a deed he slowed to be paid for.
Gladly afterwards he knew
the bull's bullness cast to the grass,
there to blast like poppies.

Lennoxbrook

For births the women figured
outside on the farm,
no longer henwives nor
the keeps of runts and orphan-lambs.

In Corley's field one day
a giant Friesian, Freda,
shouldered complications.
My sister cried

but men were busy;
In emergencies
the boys were men
and so I tugged the rope.

The lambs I'd pulled slid slick
as sea-weed from the womb
but a tractor hooked with meat-hooks
heaved on her all morning.

Eventually
the shape of calf was slung aside
to try to save the cow.
A dog had carried dead pups

for a week and lived,
but it was not the day.
Prayers nor holy water saved
the only Sunday we missed Mass.

The Rams

We called it Old Man's Beard
and the others smoked it in the barn,
its embers bright as the eyes of rams
at night in lamp-light

underneath the yew-trees
and its roots are like their horns,
the foot-and-a-half crowning the skull
or curled like a trigger.

I've watched a ram attack
and wrestle with these ends
of Witches' Rope, Honesty.
It fought until it bled.

And there they are in black and white,
the tighter wool, the horns,
of Suffolk Down and Finn,
relaxing.

They've done with tupping for the year
as the lambing happens by the house
and there's time for their feet to mend.

They stare, shudder,
recalling a rumour of anger.
They limp away and start to graze.
They go on two knees savouring the earth.

In feudal times a landlord had the 'right' to sleep with a servant girl on her wedding night. This was called

First Fruits

They were everyday together.
He followed the yardstones of water
spilt from the buckets she carried
or slipped out beyond the haggard
to the near orchard and the hens outlaying
where she gathered eggs for fairings, ribbons,
out beyond sight.

They stepped out for four years,
kitchen-girl and stable-boy,
and yet he hardly knew if
she was a woman until the day
they raced the rain to shelter
and found above the bower
a makeshift bed, brief ecstacies.

Big with a prospect she went back
to cheat her master of first fruits.
She would move to please him on the night
her groom would be distracted.
Then he'd know a secret he'd not tell
and afterwards be wanting.
But there there was not love nor trust

to let one sleep deeply beside the other
but an old order, a habit, booty,
like light from stars that have ceased
to shine. He wondered nonetheless if she could
be presentable . . . a year abroad, refinement . . .
then if she'd want to be,
if money talked louder than liking,

as he recalled their night,
her bare arms at the churning,
her blushes as she ushered in
an agent, other gentry, or as she served
at table, her apron fragrant with
the cutlings she would bring
to decorate the quarters.

The Bulls I Think

When I took the goat across country,
survived bogfall to meet the buck,
returning safe and asked to tell
I said the ram mounted my pet
and whispered in her ear
that she'd have kid.

We kept no bull;
A goat's a goat
but bulls were serious.

When we led a cow one early night
beyond Moynalty to Bell's bull
and I watched from the gate
his power swell
and the rough casual shoves
there was nothing I could add.

As if we'd helped to wound the cow
we ambled home the long acre
but every step I thought
Whatever's wrong with that beast
isn't right,

for the bulls you'd see
at Virginia Fair
or the Kells Mart of a Monday
they contained themselves.
Skin was enough and a cover.

Now the bulls I think
are quiet, not hooves
breaking the stalls of rage
but images of slow temper,
bullying grunts and the slumps of meat.

Killer

Some said that it was punishment,
a man made outside marriage
and beyond benediction —
they kept the maiden name
to gain a legacy of land
a few townlands away.

They're saying now, Jim Heaney,
there was but one bull that you feared;
it only had to wait.
As dogs in packs revert to form
bad blood smells good
and for that moment you'd have wished it

blurred by rain in a field's far corner
or winning prizes at the shows, or you
taking your ease at home by the fire.
Like butts of paling-posts the horns
strained its own body, ropes and ties;
it jabbed, jerked, split you into two fair halves.

A life uncharmed rang loud as an anthem.
The heavy feet pounded what had just been
a man. Now your half-brother repeats
'He did despite to none
but that's a brocky beast, a killer,
caged or confiscated, breeds its kind again.'

Victim

They come to a gap
and pause like sheep;
it is right —
they are sheep.

John Reilly says you'd herd
the salmon like sheep
in past times in the Blackwater
and so they swim eventually

a white current through the bushes,
the lambs at their sides
afraid of the future.
They'll pass rich grass

that hoards a skull
and nibble bald acres.
We've found them starved
in a full field

frozen numb in a nest they made.
Beside Carnbawn one evening
wind starched our scarves
and we watched

tired rams and raddled ewes
huddle against bad weather,
God's weird mood.
They abandoned their ways

that hugged the hill
as tight as rope a kicking cow;
misliking the night
they folded against its mists and shades.

There was one nearby
in bits in a ditch,
a worm at the eye,
and the dark getting used to itself.

Anniversary

A 30lb pike in the hall
from the day the men
told a serving-girl
that they were after whale

and she believed
and broadcast their success —
stay easy Ahab, Queequeg, Ishmael,
today on Mullagh lake

I must believe
that fish are mythical, or fly,
or climbed the island trees
for there's P Clarke

and even he's not caught deadbait
though shyly tells
again he won first prize
on competition day

'I'd them tethered a month
and fed on brown bread
and had only to draw them in.'
The day's too bright,

the wave's not right
or something means nothing.
The cormorant is leaving.
It's later a gentlewoman tells

it's August 15th
and we shouldn't be out
for years ago the one man drowned
and another is due to the same waters.

We walk the land
safe until
again we sail frail boats
in the unearthly destinies.

Legend

At Fore the water flows uphill,
won't boil and wood won't burn.
No living men could raise that lintel
and God knows how the abbey stands at all —
fast on a scraw
no known architecture proves its stay.

At Kieran's well a rock-seat cures your back
and something else your warts, all ills.
Mid-night, the vigil of the feast,
a pair of trout appears,
but who'd be there another night
and of course you'd court the devil

if you disbelieved at Fore.
Before the first god some god was.
Who'd tear a rosary of faith
and not a rumoured gain.
The man is wise who'll not ask why,
who'll not explain.

The Speaking Stones

There were four flags upright,
three in living memory,
a local oracle.
Now there is one, big as a door,
another low like a coffin-lid.

If cattle strayed they told the way,
or lifted lids of the evil eye,
as sure a cure as a Keogh-man's blood;
They pointed to the lost, stolen, dispossessed,
answered but once, their only clause.

A weary pilgrim, mindless of that condition
and their answer, asked again.
Their lips were sealed forever after,
their incantations over as the fair at Fore.

There are legends one can't argue with:
The agent Blaney ordered help
to break the stones to ease the plough
and was refused, 'It's poor fate
will befall the man . . .'.

He took the sledge to strike
and learned his child had drowned
in the lower meadow southward.

No crows still build on Gallow's Hill
and the lake is called Lough Rua
where flowed the blood of rebels
and still in the richest field around
are the stones tongue-tied
in the townland they've given their name.

Finding the Dead

My uncle Peter went to bed
when he heard the dowser
said he charged a fee. And that
was that. In his day men just came,
walked here and there until the rod
sprung to the stream despite themselves,
small talked and went away.

'There's three springs there',
said Brian Keelan and then stood
beyond the new dairy.
A spade dug earth, gravel, mud.
And he asked his fee,
is asking yet I'd say.
My uncle paid for what was earned.

That man found more than water.
He found a friend's gold ring
when it was hidden by St. Anthony,
found anything that strayed,
and found the dead.
Not by dredging nor combing
hills, field and forest,

not by firing over the water
nor floating loaves and mercury,
he found the dead,
the lost unentered in God's acre.
Small bits of news,
a piece of clothing — these were clues.
A weight swung like a pendulum

above a map to trace a soul.
Attention full and deep as prayer,
the plumb line swayed as if
a breath fanned and informed him.
He'd point
and there you'd look and find.
That's how they tracked

the bodies in the Blackwater
after all else had failed.

Once he failed himself,
a little girl in Donegal
erred from sight forever
while almost still within it.
That was the mystery

dark as the pool
he sees her in
and which no search can fathom.
In time the unfound dead
will gather in the maps,
will congregate in rituals of recovery
and grow up from their root in him.

On the Road

We drove south to Northampton.
As we came back
we passed a 'possum,
the first I'd ever seen.
I wanted to stop, study, and then to kill

to save its pain when I saw the bruise.
Tim thought it was all right,
spoke of their fame for faking.
Well, that's a master, I considered,
it's even bleeding.

But I'd heard of that legend earned:
one that was hurt and too young
to have learned, by a long vein
of instinct, turned on its back,
corrected, rolled over again.

Its serious snout, its flesh
like a pig's skin prepared for the knife,
prey safe as otters, a wisp of snipe.
Pig? Rat? I didn't know
and yet of all my new creatures —

snakes in the rockery, skunks, woodchucks,
chipmonks — this one by some trickery
engages my memory today on the road
as its bare, prehensile tail
clung and unchanged in the ages.

A Child of God

He might have been a Home-boy
or a love child
the way they spoke about him.
They had told me so much
we might have been acquainted —
all he did was food for talk.

An innocent or natural, his half
wit knew the neighbours' stock
and not his own;
The shuffled herds that strayed
he dealt as if by instinct.
His plain cunning reported,

once he spied his goats' big spins,
their milk to the ground,
and topped the creamery cans with it.
This scheme was graded 'A'.
In any pub's pack he was joker
but he was funnier in talk

than fact. My laughter choked
the night we met — the crooked gait,
the slobbering tales, the huge handshake,
the butt of mischief and meanness.
I twisted from their goading,
pathetic.

The goats were shot and skinned
before he knew. 'I h-h-heard a whimper
it was the man that makes the tambourines . . .'
It was. I'd seen those hides
stretched to dry
and lying in the lime that loosens hair.

And so, though you'll not read,
I offer this, Larry,
in shame and gratitude
for the parable that prompts me to remind
the pure, the perfect, the elegant, the vain,
to be as you are, to be kind.

Herding

Sometimes I watch rabbits for ages,
the light catching stones
or the edge of Lough Sheelin,
the patterns of rain,
the settlers' view —
whatever illfits our dark regard.

Proof-reading the herds
we're out to find errors,
the lame or sick, the dying or dead,
crows waving away.
They've worked flesh clean
and left warm bones.

I'm watching a lamb these days,
its mouth deformed by orf,
a lie to gentleness.
Like a girl by a mirror
and shy of a scar
it tries to run to prove its strength

shielding its face downhill on a path,
a train on a track and out of control;
we treat it anyway.
The culled, uncunning lambs,
the headbent wethers, rams,
the ewes as passive still

as in their brief mixed moment —
our horses' shadows dwarf a dozen
as we come upon them
over the mountain,
out of the ditches,
or simply from behind,

the start of a myth
for them to repeat in their pained cries
if they could remember more
than a gap that has caught them before
for we're huge and devoted
to their good.

The Positive Season

Minding the herds
we'll pass hundreds in health
and tend to two,
or count ten score
and care for a couple,
the couple not there,
the one on its back,
another in wire,
the warden's fortune.

We're surgeons, saviours,
sorrowers . . .
A ewe in a ditch,
her blind, infected head,
we lopped an ear and lanced
the skull with a cold razor
and hands cold from the rain.
Her dumb complaisance
went left in circles walking the pain.

Later she grazed
and we knew she'd survive.
Midweek she died,
slipped in a stream and drowned.
A goat's stung eye, the cries
that verged on madness rending
the afternoon, the healing sting of
vinegar, the dog packs at the herds,
the obscenities of crows, red water . . .

all, all the pitiful stations.

But this is the positive season,

though loss is expected,
a part of the whole,
the breeches, abortions
accepted, it's minor,
the primary pulse is new.
And this is their private act,
achieved without clamour or ceremony,
the herd kind alone

deep in a barn or out in a corner

composing first lambs,
the first she's ever seen.
A calm and expert innocence appears
and she goes on
trailing scarves of afterbirth.
One moans for others' young,
her instinct premature,
but minutes afterwards her lambs
home to a teat and rounded bag.

Jumble the pairs,
they don't know their own.
Mayhem, alarm, a muddle,
for an hour or two,
then out to the fields
to strengthen for slaughter,
their futures ordained,
routines underway,
already the larger, enduring herd.

Company

I wanted one
and one was dark and one was fair
but I'd learned never split a pair
except in poker,

and so they came,
across the mountain, waifs to home.
I cleared a shed, fixed posts,
tied knots they wouldn't know.

My first dam died of bloat,
the rumen paralyzed, she lost the will
to live. Poor Richard's failed to mend
on whiskey, egg whites, linseed oil.

So I'd to learn again
the trees and shrubs to skirt —
laburnum, laurel, yew,
rhododendron dying,

to mind the times for others —
the oak that binds, the ash that loosens.
One discovered echo
and bounced her call against the wall

to draw the one that answered.
As one starts from a shadow
or reflection and finds that shape
substantiated he appeared,

a scrawny buck that tired of cattle,
a rover in season
unwanted even by Jack Balfe
who feared the skin itself would smell

and not return the proper tone.
I thought to cut or squeeze
and leave him travel lighter
until he went, just as he came,

one evening suddenly.
Come near, my Toggenburgs, I say,

so you're the poor man's cow
and I'm the man;

Stay near, I say to them, farragoes
of fun, fear, friendship together,
my innocents, living whole lives
at the end of their tether.

Colaiste Oideachais Mhuire Gan Smal
Luimneach

Fallow

To hear the old men speak
of the Bluebell Wood or Ferny Field
is to chance on something holy
but I thought these were only names,
Deerfield, Deerpark, Buckminster,
until we came upon them.

I'd seen outliers from hunts
but here in a medium of meadow
they moved in concert as much at home
as otters in water, hawks in the air,
a well-known secret, adrift unminded,
past paddock and three gates.

Far from the breecher beasts around
they'd pause at an opening for hours
before entering to eat,
and these never left this park
in a handful of families' times.
Once they were rendered tame by frequent

visitations, then wary of hounds, snares,
poachers' lights, and the keeper's beat
fallen short of their runways, broken ground,
and innocent of crooked will,
like a field untilled,
knew only to seed among themselves.

Someday in Winter I'll watch
the old collapse at their loving
and a new buck continue a cycle
begun with the shedding of velvet
as light as their courage
or the step of their young.

The Darker Arts

I whittled pegs for snares,
fixed ties and nicked a twig
to hold the noose in place,
then traced the rabbits' tracks,
set with September suns
and came back in the morning.

The darker arts revived
the evenings after Martinmas.
We walked as drunks in darkness
through a muddy meadow
and talked in whispers
like dealers far from fairs even,

worked up the stream
to where the jacks had rooted beds,
our lamp-lights rippling
like small cloudy moons,
arched over our calm prey
and poised the gaff.

First was the one that got away.
A pull misjudged,
the trout dropped in the cress,
swam back. John Joe's
first words — a curse.
The others stayed.

O this was a kettle we watched
and it was boiling, those nights
the restless cattle gave us warnings,
occasions that reserved
one eye for the spotlight,
another for the bailiffs.

By woods we went also
as quietly as ribbonmen or rapparees,
a company that culled
the fallow herd by moonlight,
that rustled rivers,
tempted and trapped foxes,

and that tonight would light with lamps
game bellies in the trees
and fire single shots.
A plover stirred, badgers
scenting from afar assumed
the pale of their neat setts.

Our steady arms, our true attention,
in touch and step with our fathers —
we mimed their primal hunts,
the wiles of foxes as they dizzied hens,
the stoat's dance stunning rabbits,
the ratting packs at harvest's end.

That was the craft that we upheld
as we tramped home
and dawn enlarged to histories
we re-told, to the resonance of fish
flicking on the banks, the flutter
of wildfowl falling from the branches.

A Main

We drove down back-roads to the town
the time that wildlife thinks its own;
The meeting place was outside Mass,
rounded up, the fowl gone on.

A crowd began by word of mouth
and waited for the leader
who drew a flying funeral
across five counties to the border.

A man emerged from behind bushes,
nodded, pointed, little more.
We broke a path through fields of hay
to where sacks hung on trees and crowed.

The weights were matched, eleven paired,
by giving here and taking there,
the wings were trimmed and then were fixed
spurs to stubs of Nature's spur.

'Where's it to be?' 'In yon South field'.
Our accents argued at the gate.
A pair was carried to the pit,
the circle closed, men called their bet.

The Squire Cromwell banned this sport,
the sport of kings whose battles royal
left only one of all were pooled
at pattern, wake or festival.

And it began, a flailing lunge
of Irish Grey and big Blue Hackle,
their instincts teased struck down and down
towards cut combs and dubbed wattles.

Each time a tangled pair was parted
we looked for blood upon the beak
that bubbled from a wound below
or pierced the opposition's neck.

Their handler was an elder man
who called each ward of his Rosie.

His looked the story of a man
who loves a thing and sees it die.

Blood stained his cheek. He shook the cocks
to startle strength, sucked to the heart
to clear the lungs, spat blood and waited
for the ache he knew if they were hurt.

Ours called a draw and was turned down,
began a count of ten by ten
walking the pit to split the fight;
the bird recovered, rallied, won,

won several and the betting slowed,
the men of Larne had little,
they turned embarrassed from the pit
to double at toss-pits their pittance.

It ended early after noon.
A fisherman made fishing-flies
by footmarks, feathers, signs of battling,
old and ageing rivalries.

'El Dorado'

The accordianist began
and slowly a band foregathered,
and slowly the dancing started too,
the usual couples courageous,

the women in dresses, the men in suits
weighing the wish and the likelihood.
It was a country dance, the parish priest
was there. The bar ensured a crowd.

Some polka-ed in the foxtrot and 'trotted
in the waltz, and some were jiving expertly.
The girl in the green dress's slips
were showing; she held her handbag as she danced.

Some quickstepped in the slow sets, but those
that found their own kind in the dark danced
close in gestic heaven and learned their loving
in the backs of cars in laneways until dawn.

And some came late and argued for reductions;
others hunted others' passes, straightening up.
One was so drunk he couldn't sit down,
he knelt for the National Anthem

propped by friends, and then drove home.
Next morning in McShane's I asked
if Patsy Boylan had enjoyed the dance
and he replied, 'I don't know. Was I at it?'

The Cardplayers

They're dealing in twos and threes
the corner-crumpled cards
that draw the pennies, half-pennies,
to the board. It's evening,
Saturday, and their work's done.

That man has sheep beyond the mill,
and that works land his fathers owned,
a labourer. That man alone can boast
he made his tools, and that does anything
and is happiest at nothing.

It's this one says 'You know,
there's four Michaels sat down
to this game'.
                    The youngest
is circling his chair to change his luck
when in she comes;

She has followed her legend into the parish
to ruffle his hair and whisper wildly
'I'll be your luck. Let you win there
and later we'll together prize.'
The others laugh, ask who's to deal. He plays to win.

Mare

Perhaps the horse dreams too
you find in the morning
awake in a flower of sweat.

In a far country they say
face to face with a horse at night
spit across your left shoulder.

At home they'd pack a pillow
with straw to satisfy the mare,
but there three times

with her wedding ring
my mother would cross
a sty in your eye

and if that didn't cure it
it wasn't a sty.
A doorkey hung above the bed

is certain sleep
and a night as still
as a stone tied round their necks

or all the horses hobbled.
May the mare near you be the one
that loses its shoe by your door.

Colaiste Oideachais Mhuire Gan Smal
Luimneach